Sara Swan Miller

Flies

From Flower Flies to Mosquitoes

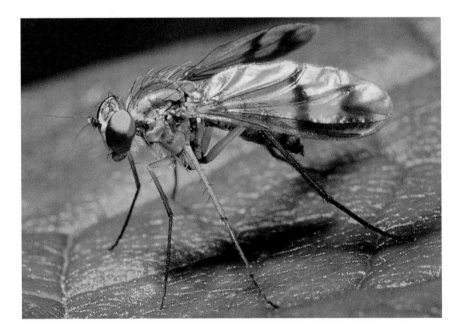

Franklin Watts - A Division of Grolier Publishing
New York • London • Hong Kong • Sydney • Danbury, Connecticut

For Ann Guenther, who would make a great fly watcher

Photographs ©: BBC Natural History Unit: 5 top right (John Heidecker), 5 bottom left (Mark & Juliet Yates); Billy Beatty: 7 bottom; Dr. E. R. Degginger: cover, 13, 25, 27, 33, 43; Frederick D. Atwood: 6; Photo Researchers: 15 (Ken Brate), 37 (James Prince), 17 (Harry Rogers), 35 (Mich Summer); Steve Marshall: 1, 5 top left, 19, 21, 23, 29, 31, 39; Visuals Unlimited: 7 top (R.F. Ashley), 41 (Bill Beatty), 5 bottom right (Gustay Verderber); Walter Gould: 40.

Illustrations by Jose Gonzales and Steve Savage

Visit Franklin Watts on the Internet at:
http://publishing.grolier.com

Library of Congress Cataloging-in-Publication Data

Miller, Sara Swan.
Flies: From flower flies to mosquitoes / Sara Swan Miller.
    p. cm. — (Animals in order)
    Includes bibliographical references and index.
    Summary: An introduction to flies, a taxonomic order of insects that includes descriptions of fourteen species and recommendations for finding, identifying, and observing them.
    ISBN 0-531-11486-4 (lib.bdg.)   0-531-15919-1 (pbk.)
    1. Diptera—Juvenile literature. 2. Diptera—Classification—Juvenile literature.
[1. Flies.]   I. Title.   II. Series.
QL533.2.M55   1998
595.77—dc21
                                                    97-24035
                                                       CIP
                                                        AC

Contents

Is That *Really* a Fly?

"There's a fly in my soup!"
"What are those big flies doing over that pond?"
"Why is that fly fluttering against the window?"

Have you ever heard people say things like this? How did they know they were really looking at flies? Many people think that any small creature that flies must be a fly. Not always!

Flies are actually a special group of insects. They are different from bees, butterflies, and other flying insects.

Would you like to become a fly expert? This is your chance! On the next page are four "flies." But only one is *really* a fly. Do you know which one?

1. Firefly

2. Crane fly

3. Dragonfly

4. Mayfly

Traits of a Fly

Crane fly

And the answer is . . . number 2! How can you tell?

First, and most important, flies have only one pair of wings. All the other insects have two pairs. Instead of a second pair of wings, flies have two small, club-like structures called *halteres*.

Flies are the best fliers in the insect world. They can fly very fast and turn very easily. Their wings may beat up to 1,000 times a minute! Many flies can hover, spin, and even fly backward. How do they do that? The secret behind a fly's amazing flying abilities is its halteres. Sense organs at the base of the halteres tell the fly whether it's on course. They also help the fly balance while it flies.

Flies grow in four stages. First, a female lays eggs. In most species, the *larvae* that hatch are called *maggots*. Maggots come in all sizes, shapes, and colors. They feed and grow and shed their skins—then they feed and grow some more. After maggots shed their skins for the last time, they rest as *pupae*. While they rest, they change into adults.

A fly's mouth is made for sucking liquid foods. Many flies have mouthparts that are also good for piercing and lapping. Inside their heads are one or two strong pumps made of muscle. These let flies suck juice from plants, animals, and other food.

As a group, flies feed on just about anything. Some suck nectar or other plant juices, some eat manure or sewage, and some suck juices from other insects. Many feed on other animals, both dead and alive—including humans. Others may enjoy *mucus*, fungi, and even wine. Whatever there is to eat, you can be sure that there's a kind of fly out there that wants to eat it!

Flesh fly maggots

Giant robberfly with a moth

The Order of Living Things

A tiger has more in common with a house cat than with a daisy. A scorpion is more like a butterfly than a jellyfish. Scientists arrange living things into groups based on how they look and how they act. A tiger and a house cat belong to the same group, but a daisy belongs to a different group.

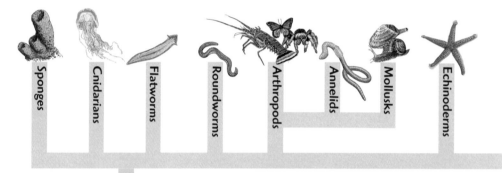

Sponges · Cnidarians · Flatworms · Roundworms · Arthropods · Annelids · Mollusks · Echinoderms

Animals

Plants · Fungi

Protists

Monerans

All living things can be placed in one of five groups called *kingdoms:* the plant kingdom, the animal kingdom, the fungus kingdom, the moneran kingdom, or the protist kingdom. You can probably name many of the creatures in the plant and animal kingdoms. The *fungus* kingdom includes mushrooms, yeasts, and molds. The moneran and protist kingdoms contain thousands of living things that are too small to see without a microscope.

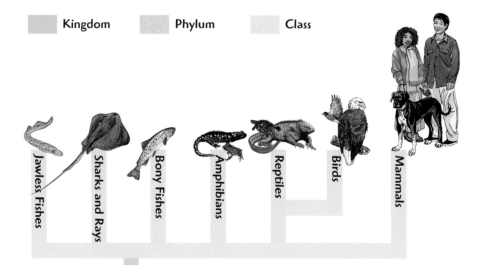

Kingdom   Phylum   Class

Jawless Fishes

Sharks and Rays

Bony Fishes

Amphibians

Reptiles

Birds

Mammals

Chordates

Because there are millions and millions of living things on Earth, some of the members of one kingdom may not seem all that similar. The animal kingdom includes creatures as different as tarantulas and trout, jellyfish and jaguars, salamanders and sparrows, elephants and earthworms.

To show that an elephant is more like a jaguar than an earthworm, scientists further separate the creatures in each kingdom into more specific groups. The animal kingdom can be divided into nine *phyla*. Humans belong to the chordate phylum. Almost all chordates have a backbone.

Each phylum can be subdivided into many *classes*. Humans, mice, and elephants all belong to the mammal class. Each class can be further divided into *orders*; orders into *families*, families into *genera*, and genera into *species*. All of the members of a species are very similar.

How Flies Fit In

You can probably guess that the flies belong to the animal kingdom. They have much more in common with spiders and snakes than with maple trees and morning glories.

Flies belong to the arthropod phylum. All arthropods have a tough outer skin. Can you guess what other living things might be arthropods? Examples include spiders, scorpions, mites, ticks, millipedes, and centipedes. Many arthropods live in the ocean. Lobsters, crabs, and shrimps all belong to this group.

The arthropod phylum can be divided into a number of classes. Flies belong to the insect class. Butterflies, ants, and beetles are also insects.

There are thirty different orders of insects. The flies make up one of these orders. In the United States and Canada, 25 percent of all insects are flies. Flies make up the second-largest order of insects in the world, after beetles. Flies can be divided into a number of families, genera, and species.

You will learn more about some of the flies in this book. As you will soon discover, flies live in every kind of *habitat* in the world—from the tropics to the Arctic. Some may even live in your home.

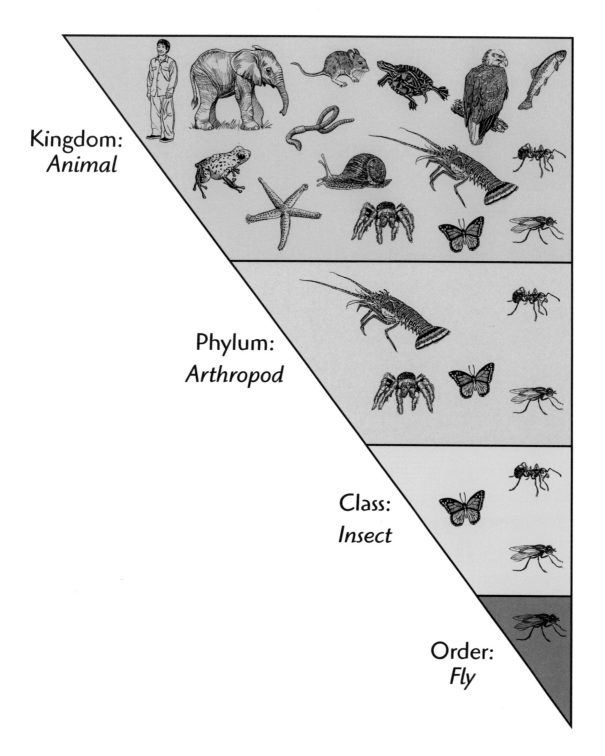

Kingdom:
Animal

Phylum:
Arthropod

Class:
Insect

Order:
Fly

Flower Flies

FAMILY: Syrphidae
COMMON EXAMPLE: Drone fly
GENUS AND SPECIES: *Eristalis tenax*
SIZE: 5/8 inch (16 mm)

You have probably seen flower flies hovering over flowers and thought they were bees or wasps. Many species of flower flies look so much like bees or wasps that it is hard to tell the difference.

These look-alikes fool birds and other *predators*, too. Some flower flies have another trick. If they do get caught, they buzz loudly to frighten off their enemy. As soon as the predator lets go, the sneaky flower fly zooms away.

Flower flies are so quick that it's hard to get a close look at them. One moment you might spot one hovering over a flower—its wings beating so fast you can't even see them. Then, all at once, it vanishes! A moment later, it is hovering over another flower.

The drone fly is a type of flower fly that looks almost exactly like a honeybee. It is the same size and has almost the same markings. It acts like a honeybee, too.

Female drone flies don't raise their young in hives, though. They lay eggs near stagnant water. Each larva, called a rat-tailed maggot, has a long tube at the end of its abdomen. It uses the tube like a snorkel to breathe when it's under water.

Bee Flies

FAMILY: Bombyliidae
COMMON EXAMPLE: Large bee fly
GENUS: *Bombylius major*
SIZE: 1/4 to 1/2 inch (6 to 13 mm)

Like flower flies, bee flies look like bees. You might see one hovering over a flower, sucking nectar through its long *proboscis*. It doesn't even have to land on the flower to get its meal.

Sometimes bee flies hover a few inches above a hot dirt road. If you get too close, they zip away so fast that they seem to vanish into thin air. Of course, looking like bees helps protect bee flies from their enemies. It helps them in another way, too. Female bee flies can lay their eggs in a bees' nest. The bees don't even notice them. When the maggots hatch, they feed on the eggs and larvae of bees.

The large bee fly looks almost exactly like a bee known as the solitary bee. The female bee fly hovers over a flower, waiting for a solitary bee to come along. Then she follows the bee back to its hive. When the bee leaves again, the large bee fly lays its eggs in the doorway.

When the tiny maggots hatch, they make their way into the bee's nest. Once they get inside, they feast on bee eggs and larvae. When the maggots grow big enough, they *pupate* inside a shell covered with strong spines. These spines help the adult bee flies break out of the hive. Then, off they go to mate and look for more solitary bees to follow home.

Tachinid Flies

FAMILY: Tachinidae
COMMON EXAMPLE: Tachina fly
GENUS AND SPECIES: *Trichopoda pennipes*
SIZE: 1/4 to 1/2 inch (6 to 13 mm)

Gardeners and farmers like tachinid flies! They fly from flower to flower sipping nectar. Like bees and butterflies, they help *pollinate* flowers, so the flowers can make new seeds.

Farmers and gardeners welcome the maggots of tachinid flies, too. They feed on farm and garden pests. Female tachinid flies lay their eggs near, on, or even inside, another insect. The unlucky insect serves as food for the tiny maggots.

Some flies lay their flat, white, oval eggs on a leaf where their victim is likely to be. The larvae crawl about until they find their *prey*.

Other flies lay eggs on the back of a caterpillar. The maggots burrow inside their victim. Still others "drill" through the outer skin of an insect and lay eggs inside the victim's body. When the larvae hatch, they eat their *host* from the inside out.

Larvae take their time eating their host. The maggots don't want to kill their prey until they are all grown up. First, they munch on the body parts that are less important for keeping the insect alive. Then they eat the victim's major organs, such as the heart. When a maggot is ready to pupate, it drills its way out of its victim and drops to the ground.

16

Farmers and forestry people often use tachinid flies rather than insect sprays to control pests like gypsy moths. The chemicals in sprays can poison helpful insects as well as the pests. These sprays don't do people any good, either. That's why you should always wash fruits and vegetables before eating them.

Fruit Flies

FAMILY: Tephritidae
COMMON EXAMPLE: Goldenrod gall fly
GENUS AND SPECIES: *Eurosta solidaginis*
SIZE: 3/8 inch (9.5 mm)

Have you ever noticed a round ball growing around the stem of a goldenrod plant? This ball is called a goldenrod ball *gall*. If you could look inside the gall, you would find a small pale maggot living there. This is the larva of the goldenrod gall fly.

How did that maggot get inside the gall? In the spring, female flies lay their eggs on the stems of goldenrods. When each larva hatches, it uses a pair of mouthhooks to dig its way into the stem.

The goldenrod seems to be annoyed by the maggot. It grows a ball-like swelling around the larva. All summer and into the fall, the maggot lives inside the gall and munches on its plant tissue. Most birds and other enemies don't even know the maggot is there. It's very safe inside its little home.

During the cold winter, the maggot *hibernates* inside its gall. When it wakes up in the spring, the larva drills a tunnel to the outside edge of the gall. It pupates inside the tunnel. The adult gall fly crawls out of the tunnel and flies off to begin the cycle again.

Not all fruit flies live inside galls. The apple maggot fly lays its eggs in the skin of fruits, such as apples and berries. The larvae tunnel into the fruit and gorge on fruit until they are ready to pupate.

House Flies

FAMILY: *Muscidae*
COMMON EXAMPLE: House fly
GENUS AND SPECIES: *Musca domestica*
SIZE: 1/8 to 1/4 inch (3 to 6 mm)

When you think of flies, you probably picture a house fly. Whether you live in the United States, India, or Timbucktu, you'll find house flies living with you. The only house where you'll never find one is an igloo!

Can you guess the secret of their success? House flies will eat almost anything! They like meat, plants, bread, and sugar. House flies are also perfectly happy to lap up blood, vomit, or animal droppings.

House fly maggots can live in any damp place, but they prefer manure piles, garbage, or dead animals. Like their parents, maggots will eat just about anything—including wet newspaper.

A house fly's eating habits are not very pretty. To soften its food, a fly vomits up a drop of liquid on it. The "vomit drop" digests the food and turns it into a liquid. Then, the fly sucks up the drop with its proboscis.

Most of the time, some of the vomit drop stays on the food it was eating. That drop contains millions of germs that the fly carried from whatever it was eating last. Maybe it just had a meal of manure or garbage, or even mucus from a sick person's handkerchief. That's why you don't want to eat anything a house fly has been eating!

Cluster Flies

FAMILY: Calliphoridae
COMMON EXAMPLE: Cluster fly
GENUS AND SPECIES: *Pollenia rudis*
SIZE: 3/8 inch (9.5 mm)

In the fall or spring, you may have noticed a crowd of flies clustering together on your windows. You probably wondered what those "house flies" were doing crawling all over your windows. You were really looking at cluster flies, not house flies.

Cluster flies do look a lot like house flies, but they are a little bigger, and they hold their wings closer together. When they first wake up from hibernation, they are also much slower-moving. House flies dart about quickly, while cluster flies are bumbling and sluggish because they are still groggy.

If you were an earthworm, you wouldn't like cluster flies at all. Adult flies mate in February, and the females lay their eggs in the *soil*. When the larvae hatch, they find an earthworm and burrow inside its body. They live there for about 2 weeks, feeding on the worm's insides. Then they come out to pupate in the soil. Finally, the adults push their way out of the soil and fly away.

So, what are cluster flies doing on your windows? In the fall, cluster flies begin to look for a place to hibernate. They creep into buildings through any hole they can find. For a while, before it gets too cold, they may bask in the sunshine on your windowsills.

During the winter, they hibernate in cracks and crevices in your walls or attic. When it warms up in spring, the cluster flies crowd around your windows, trying to get out.

Pomace Flies

FAMILY: Drosophilidae
COMMON EXAMPLE: Fruit fly
GENUS AND SPECIES: *Drosophila melanogaster*
SIZE: 1/16 inch (1.5 mm)

Have you ever seen a cloud of tiny flies hovering around your fruit bowl? Have you ever left a glass of juice on the kitchen counter and found tiny dead flies floating in it?

Pomace flies, which are sometimes called "fruit flies" or "vinegar flies," live wherever they find rotting fruit—in other words, just about anywhere in the world. They are especially fond of wineries, where they sip fine wines with gusto.

These flies can really hold their alcohol. Any other living creature would be poisoned if they drank as much as a pomace fly. These flies have special juices inside their bodies that help them digest alcohol, so wine and the juice of rotting fruits doesn't seem to affect them.

What attracts the pomace flies, though, is not the alcohol, but the yeast in the alcohol. If they can't find alcohol or yeast, they make do with fungi, slime molds, or just bacteria.

Pomace flies reproduce very quickly. Each female lays 2,000 eggs at a time, and the eggs become adults in less than 2 weeks. No wonder your fruit bowl is full of pomace flies!

Horse Flies

FAMILY: Tabanidae
COMMON EXAMPLE: American horse fly
GENUS AND SPECIES: *Tabanus americanus*
SIZE: 1/2 to 1 1/8 inch (13 to 28 mm)

Horse flies are big flies. Female horse flies are more than 1 inch (2.5 cm) long. They have big eyes, too, which can be very beautiful. They sparkle with bands and patches of rainbow colors.

One day, you may be taking a quiet walk in the woods. All at once, with no warning at all—ZAP! Something bites you hard. Horse flies can give you a really painful bite! Female horse flies need a meal of blood to make their eggs grow, and they take it from any *warm-blooded* animal that happens to cross their path.

Horse flies have powerful mouthparts that can slice and pierce through the toughest skin. They quickly lap up all the blood that flows out.

Females lay their eggs on plants that grow in wet places. After the eggs hatch, the maggots drop into the water and dine on small aquatic creatures.

Male horse flies aren't interested in sucking blood. They would rather feed on plant juices or nectar. But the next time you go for a walk in the woods, put on some insect repellent first, just in case a female is out for blood.

Fungus Gnats

FAMILY: Mycetophilidae
COMMON EXAMPLE: Fungus gnat
GENUS AND SPECIES: *Gnorista macroides*
SIZE: 1/8 to 1/4 inch (3 to 6 mm)

Fungus gnats are small flies that feed on mold, fungus, and rotting plants. The larvae of some fungus gnats have an unusual way of getting around. Hundreds of them group together and travel along the forest floor. As the group moves, it looks like a snake or a large worm slithering through the leaves. The "snake worm" is about 1 inch (2.5 cm) wide and can be up to 15 feet (4.5 m) long.

To form a "snake worm," the larvae pile on top of each other in several layers. The ones on the bottom crawl along more slowly than the ones on the top. When the maggots find themselves at the tail end of the snake worm, they crawl up on top and begin to wiggle along more quickly than their buddies. When they reach the head of their snake worm, the larvae drop down to the ground. The whole snake worm moves about 1 inch (2.5 cm) per minute.

Nobody knows why fungus gnat larvae travel this way—or where they're going. Some scientists think that they are on their way to a good place to pupate. Traveling all together as a large, scary snake may protect them from their enemies. As the saying goes, there's safety in numbers!

Dance Flies

FAMILY: Empididae
COMMON EXAMPLE: Dance fly
GENUS: *Rhamphomyia longicauda*
SIZE: 1/8 to 1/4 inch (3 to 6 mm)

Have you ever seen a cloud of flies dancing over a pond or in a shady woodland? Their rising and falling dance looks like a graceful ballet in the air. These dancers are male dance flies trying to catch a female's attention. When a female flies in to take a closer look, the males try to capture her so they can mate.

Some male dance flies carry a gift for the female. It looks like a little balloon tucked under their legs. The males make the balloon from silk that comes from special glands on their legs. Most of the time, the female will find a tasty insect inside. This is the only food the adult female will eat. After she eats her treat, the flies mate.

Other males are sneaky. They give the female a package with nothing inside. The male mates with the female while she's busy unwrapping what she thinks is a lovely present. This seems like a nasty trick!

Female dance flies lay their eggs in damp soil or on the moist edge of a pond. The larvae eat small insects that live in the soil or in the water. During the winter, they pupate in rotting vegetation. When spring comes, the adults fly out to dance their beautiful air ballet.

Flesh Flies

FAMILY: Sarcophagidae
COMMON EXAMPLE: Pitcher plant fly
GENUS AND SPECIES: *Sarcophaga sarraceniae*
SIZE: 1/4 inch (6 mm)

The pitcher plant is unusual—it's a meat-eater. The plant's hollow leaves collect rainwater, so when an insect falls in by mistake, it drowns. Then, the pitcher plant digests it. But the larvae of the pitcher plant fly can live and grow inside the leaves with no trouble.

The female pitcher plant fly is unusual, too. It doesn't lay eggs. Instead, the larvae hatch while they're still inside their mother, and she leaves them inside the pitcher plant. They get to work right away eating the insects trapped inside—stealing the pitcher plant's dinner!

When they're ready to pupate, the larvae drill a hole in the bottom of the pitcher plant and drop to the ground. In the process, all the water drains out of the plant. The pitcher plant dies because it can't trap any more insects to feed on.

The larvae of other species of flesh flies feed on rotting flesh, dead insects, droppings, crabs, snails, and spiders. Some live and feed inside other insects. Others can be found inside sores and wounds on an animal's skin.

Some female flesh flies drop their larvae on rotting meat. If they can't get very close to the meat, these little bombers don't care. They drop their larvae from as much as 24 inches (61 cm) overhead.

Mosquitoes

FAMILY: Culicidae
COMMON EXAMPLE: House mosquito
GENUS AND SPECIES: *Culex pipiens*
SIZE: 1/8 to 1/4 inch (3 to 6 mm)

We all know a mosquito when we see one. There are more than 2,000 different species of mosquitoes, and they live all over the world —even in the Arctic. If you have a pond, pool, or even a puddle near your house, you have mosquitoes, too.

What you may not know is that some mosquitoes won't bite you. Male mosquitoes are quite happy to suck nectar from flowers. Most of the time the females feed on nectar, too. But after mosquitoes mate, the females of most species need a blood meal to help their eggs grow. Some get blood from birds. Others only like frog blood. But most mosquitoes prefer warm-blooded mammals—like you.

The mouthparts of a female mosquito have six sharp needles that are perfect for drawing blood. The mosquito uses four of the needles to cut into a victim's skin. She presses the other two needles together to make a tube that sucks up the blood.

Most mosquitoes lay their eggs on the surface of a pond, a puddle, or water inside a decaying stump or an old tire. The larvae, called wrigglers, live in the water and eat whatever comes their way. You can find them hanging head-down from the water's surface. They breathe through a tiny tube on their tails. What a perfect snorkel!

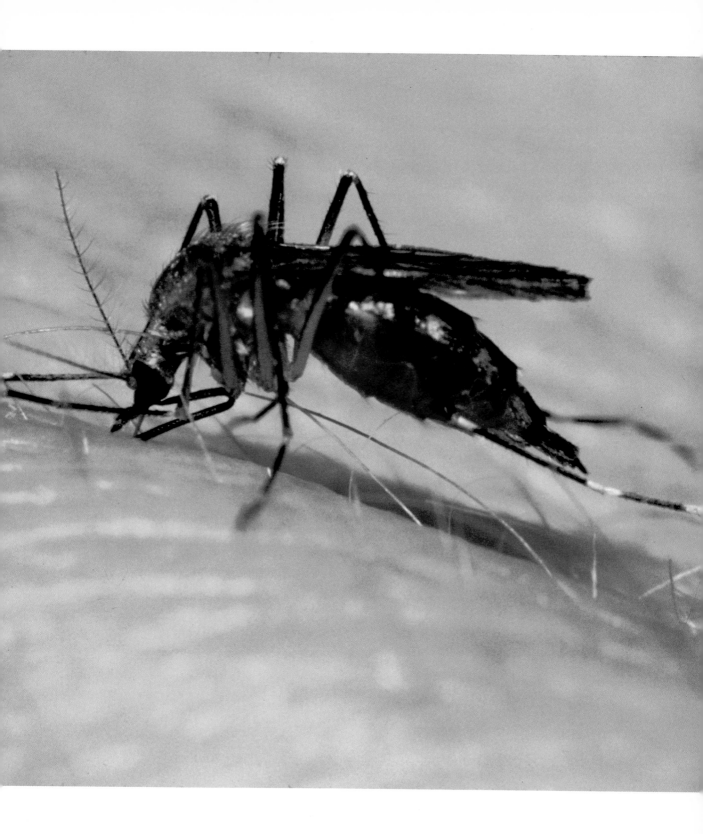

Crane Flies

FAMILY: Tipulidae
COMMON EXAMPLE: Central crane fly
GENUS AND SPECIES: *Tipula cunctans*
SIZE: 1/2 to 3/4 inch (13 to 19 mm)

Have you ever seen a giant "mosquito" creeping across your ceiling? Don't worry! Mosquitoes don't get that big. It was just a crane fly.

Crane flies can't hurt you—they don't even have biting mouth-parts. The adults of most species eat nothing at all. They only come into your house because, like moths, they fly toward lights.

You may see a swarm of crane flies floating in the air over a pond or stream. This is their mating dance. The females of most species lay eggs in ponds or streams, but some just lay them in mud. The larvae look like slugs or legless caterpillars.

If you look closely at a crane fly larva, you will see a disk at the end of its tail surrounded by tiny tubes. When it needs air, the larva sticks that disk out of the water and breathes. Most of the time, it lies on the bottom of streams or ponds, waiting for its favorite food—a tubifex worm—to wriggle by!

The larvae of one species live in grain fields and feed on the roots of the crops. People call these larvae "leather-jackets" because their skin is so tough.

Marsh Flies

FAMILY: Chironomidae
COMMON EXAMPLE: Snail-killing fly
GENUS AND SPECIES: *Poecilographa decorum*
SIZE: 1/4 to 3/8 inch (6 to 9.5 mm)

Do you like eating snails? French people do, and so do the larvae of marsh flies. They eat other small shelled animals, too. But snails and slugs are their favorites.

Some marsh fly larvae live and eat on land, while others search for their prey in water. Since they don't have gills, the larvae in ponds and streams have to stay near the surface, so they can gulp air when they need it.

These maggots have water-repellent "float hairs" around the two air holes in their tails. These hairs help them float just below the water's surface. The float hairs work so well that a larva can stay near the surface even when it is holding on to a big, heavy snail!

The larvae of some species may kill more than a dozen snails before they are ready to pupate. Others may eat only three or four. They are careful to eat the less important parts of the snail first, so that their victim will stay alive and fresh longer.

Some marsh flies prey on snails that carry *parasites*. These parasites can causes diseases in cattle and people. In Hawaii, the larvae of snail-killing flies have been used to fight these diseases.

Gardeners welcome another species of marsh fly that attacks the slugs that eat lettuce. These slug-killers lie in wait for their prey. When they feel a slug's slimy skin, they crawl inside and eat the slug from the inside out. They are the guardians of the lettuce patch!

How to Be a Fly Watcher

A lot of people enjoy bird-watching, but how many fly watchers are there in the world? You can invent a new hobby! All you need is a hand lens that magnifies three times.

It's a good idea to take along a notebook and pencil, too, so you can write down what you find and draw pictures. You might also want to carry an insect field guide to identify the flies you see.

If you were a beetle watcher or a bug watcher, you could collect the insects you find in jars. But flies could get hurt inside a jar. Like a bird-watcher, you will use just your eyes and ears to go fly-watching.

Begin your search in a local garden or meadow. Look for bee flies and flower flies hovering over flower blossoms. The flies may look like bees or wasps, but you'll be able to tell the difference if you watch their movements closely. Flower flies usually hover over a flower, while bees dive right in. Flower flies also zip around much faster than bees and wasps.

Look for the flat, white, oval eggs of tachinid flies on the backs of caterpillars. Search for galls on the leaves and stems of plants. If you find a goldenrod gall, you'll know there is a gall fly larvae living inside. If you come across animal droppings or a dead animal, look to see if there are any flies cleaning it up. (Don't get too close—and hold your nose if you have to.)

Before you go looking for flies in the woods, it's a good idea to put some insect repellent on your clothes. You probably won't have any trouble finding mosquitoes or horse flies. Search for fungus gnats on mushrooms. You might even see them traveling along the forest floor as a "snake worm." Look for dance flies, too, performing their air ballet. If you're very lucky, you may find pitcher plants growing in damp places with pitcher plant fly larvae swimming around inside.

Useful Tools

Two white plastic washtubs

A sieve about 8 inches (20 cm) across

A few clear plastic jars

A tablespoon

A field guide to pond and stream life

Ponds and streams are great places for fly watching. Take along some equipment to help you search for fly larvae in the water.

When you get to the water, fill one of the tubs with water. Fly larvae that live in ponds and streams can't survive for very long out of water. Use the sieve to scoop mud or gravel from the bottom and put it in the other tub. Then, use your spoon to gently search through the muck. If you find a fly larva, put it into the tub.

It's easy to spot crane fly larvae—they look like large, legless caterpillars. Can you see the breathing disk at the end of their tails? Look for tiny marsh fly larvae just below the surface of the pond. You may even find mosquito "wrigglers" dangling from the surface. Use your sieve to capture them and put them in the tub of water.

Of course, many of the larvae you find will be other kinds of insects. Can you figure out which ones are fly larvae? To get a closer look, put your samples in one of the jars along with some water. Can you identify them with the help of a hand lens and a field guide?

Be on the lookout for adult flies, too. Mosquitoes and dance flies may be swarming over the water's surface. You might also see a cloud of huge crane flies floating in the air.

You can even be a fly watcher in the comfort of your home. You can't miss house flies and cluster flies. Maybe you also have some pomace flies living with you.

Whenever you spot a fly, write down what you see and draw a picture. If you watch them closely, you may discover something that no one has ever noticed before. You can become a fly expert!

Words to Know

class—a group of creatures within a phylum that share certain characteristics.

family—a group of creatures within an order that share certain characteristics.

fungus (plural **fungi**)—one of the five kingdoms of living things. Fungi obtain nutrients from decaying plant and animal matter.

gall—a swelling created by a plant when a gall insect lays her eggs in it, or when it is infected with certain bacteria or fungi.

genus (plural **genera**)—a group of creatures within a family that share certain characteristics.

habitat—the environment where a plant or animal lives and grows.

haltere—one of a pair of small, knobbed structures that flies have instead of hind wings. They contain sense organs that help in flight.

hibernate—to spend the winter in a resting state, with slowed heart rate and breathing.

host—a creature that serves as a home and source of food for a smaller creature.

kingdom—one of the five divisions into which all living things are placed: the animal kingdom, the plant kingdom, the fungus kingdom, the moneran kingdom, and the protist kingdom.

larva (plural **larvae**)—a newly hatched insect in the second stage of insect metamorphosis.

maggot—the larva of a fly.

mucus—a slimy material produced by the mucus membranes. Mucus that comes from the nose is called snot.

order—a group of creatures within a class that share certain characteristics.

parasite—a creature that invades another creature and uses its victim's body for its own benefit.

phylum (plural **phyla**)—a group of creatures within a kingdom that share certain characteristics.

pollinate—to transfer pollen (the male sex cells of a green plant) from the anther (male part of a flower) to the stigma (female part of a flower). The pollen may be carried from one flower to another by insects, birds, bats, or the wind.

predator—an animal that hunts and eats other animals.

prey—an animal hunted for food by another animal (a predator).

proboscis—a long, tubelike mouth for sucking.

pupa (plural **pupae**)—the third stage of insect metamorphosis, usually a resting stage, when the larvae turn into adults.

pupate—to change into an adult.

soil—the layer of dirt and other material on the upper surface of the ground.

species—a group of creatures within a genus that share certain characteristics. Members of a species can mate and produce young.

warm blooded—a creature that can regulate its internal body temperature.

Learning More

Books

Booth, Jerry. *Big Bugs*. San Diego: Harcourt Brace, 1994.

Cottam, Clarence. *Insects: A Golden Guide*. Racine, WI: Western Publishing Co., 1987.

Ganeri, Anita. *Insects*. New York: Franklin Watts, 1993.

Johnson, Sylvia A. *Water Insects*. Minneapolis: Lerner Publications, 1989.

Leahy, Christopher. *Peterson's First Guide to Insects*. Boston: Houghton Mifflin, 1987.

Mound, Laurence. *Amazing Insects*. New York: Knopf, 1993.

CD-ROM

Bug Adventure: An Insect Adventure. Knowledge Adventure, 1995.

Web Sites

The Bug Club Page has a list of insect experts that you can contact by e-mail. The club also organizes local field trips and publishes a newsletter six times a year.
http://www.ex.ac.uk/bugclub

The Young Entomologist's Society Page runs a program called "Bugs-On-Wheels." You may be able to arrange for an insect expert to visit your school and show your classmates some really cool insects.
http://insects.ummz.lsa.umich.edu/yes/yes.html

Index

About the Author

Sara Swan Miller has enjoyed working with children all her life, first as a Montessori nursery school teacher, and later as an outdoor environmental educator at the Mohonk Preserve in New Paltz, New York. As the director of the Preserve school program, she has led hundreds of children on field trips and taught them the importance of appreciating and respecting the natural world, especially its less lovable "creepy crawlies."

She has written a number of children's books including *Three Stories You Can Read to Your Dog*; *Three Stories You Can Read to Your Cat*; *What's in the Woods?: An Outdoor Activity Book*; *Oh, Cats of Camp Rabbitbone!*; *Piggy in the Parlor and Other Tales*; *Better Than TV*; and *Will You Sting Me? Will You Biter Me? The Truth About Some Scary-Looking Insects*.

DATE			